Why Do Birds Sing?

by JOAN HOLUB

illustrations by Anna DiVito

Dial Books for Young Readers • New York

Published by Dial Books for Young Readers
A division of Penguin Young Readers Group

345 Hudson Street
New York, New York 10014
Text copyright © 2004 by Joan Holub
Illustrations copyright © 2004 by Anna DiVito

Printed in China

The Dial Easy-to-Read logo is a registered trademark of
Dial Books for Young Readers, a division of Penguin Young Readers Group
® TM 1,162,718.

1 3 5 7 9 10 8 6 4 2

LIBRARY OF CONGRESS CATALOGING-IN-PUBLICATION DATA:
Holub, Joan.
Why do birds sing? / by Joan Holub; illustrations by Anna DiVito.
p. cm.
ISBN 0-8037-2999-5 (hardcover)—ISBN 0-14-240106-4 (pbk.)
1. Birds—Miscellanea—Juvenile literature. [1. Birds—Miscellanea.
2. Questions and answers.] I. DiVito, Anna, ill. II. Title.
QL676.2.H65 2004
598—dc22   2003064945

ISBN 0-8037-2999-5

Reading Level 3.0

Photo Credits

Front Cover, pages 1, 12, 14, 17 (parrot), 24–26, 29, 33, 34, 41, 43, 45; copyright ©
Dorling Kindersley; page 5 copyright © Gail Shumway/Getty Images, Inc.; pages 6, 11, 21,
27; copyright © Corel; page 7 copyright © PhotoDisc Inc.; page 8 copyright © Robert A.
Tyrell Photography; pages 9, 15, 37 copyright © PictureQuest; page 10 copyright © Gay
Bumgarner/Getty Images Inc.; page 17 (pelican) copyright © National Geographic Image
Collection; page 19 copyright © Tom McHugh/Photo Researchers Inc.; page 23 copyright
© Tom & Pat Leeson/Photo Researchers Inc.; page 28 copyright © Fritz Prenzel; page 31
copyright © W. Lynn Seldon Jr./Omni-Photo Communications, Inc.; page 35 copyright
© Digital Vision; page 39 copyright © Getty Images, Inc.; page 40 copyright ©
Paul McCormick/Getty Images, Inc.; page 48 copyright © Dynamic Graphics

Note: The information in this book is not complete and is not intended to provide professional advice
regarding appropriate care, food, housing, toys, or games for your pet, or advice concerning the suitabili-
ty of any of these pets for your family. Consult experts at your pet store, organizations that educate about
birds, and your vet for more complete information about the pets in this book before purchasing these
pets or any supplies for them. Always wash your hands before and after handling a bird or its cage. Birds
may bite, scratch, carry disease, or provoke allergic reactions. Consult your doctor in the event of injury
or allergic reaction. It is inadvisable to tame many wild birds to become pets. Review state, city, and local
laws in your area before purchasing any bird, since it may be illegal to own some of the birds mentioned
in this book in some locations.

For Rena Bidwell, a wonderful neighbor—J.H.

For Remi and Brianna—A.D.

Do you like birds?

Birds are interesting
and fun to watch.
Some birds are friendly
and make great pets.
Popular pet birds include
the parakeet, finch, parrot, canary,
and cockatiel (KAHK-uh-teel).

Parrots

Black-Crowned Crane

How many different kinds of birds are there?

There are over 9,000 kinds of birds.

Sparrows, robins, and pigeons

are some well-known wild birds.

Birds live in cities, forests, marshlands,

deserts, mountains, and everywhere else

in the world.

Pigeon

Bee Hummingbird

What are the smallest and biggest birds?

The bee hummingbird
weighs as little as a dime and
lays eggs the size of peas!
An ostrich can grow up to nine feet tall
and weigh 345 pounds!
It lays fifteen to twenty eggs at a time.
Each egg is about seven inches long.

Ostrich

Why do birds have feathers?

Birds are the only animals with feathers.
Feathers keep birds warm and dry
and help them fly.
Some birds have feathers that are
brightly colored to attract mates.
A male bird's feathers are usually
more colorful than a female's feathers.

Female Cardinal

Male Cardinal

Owl

Feathers with colors and patterns
that look like the surrounding area
help protect a bird by hiding it.
This is called camouflage (CAM-o-flahj).

How do birds fly?

Birds have light, hollow bones
and strong chest muscles.
The shape and movement
of their feathered wings
beating against the air help to lift birds.
Once they are in the air,
most birds must flap their wings to fly.

Parakeet

Some birds can glide, soar, or hover

when conditions are right.

An albatross can glide in the air

for hours without flapping its wings.

An eagle can soar on moving air currents.

A hummingbird hovers in place

by moving its wings about seventy times

every second!

Can all birds fly?

Most birds can fly.

Some birds, such as chickens,

can fly only a few feet at a time.

The great bustard is the

heaviest bird that is able to fly.

It weighs up to forty-two pounds.

But not all birds fly.

The ostrich, kiwi, and penguin

are some birds that can't fly.

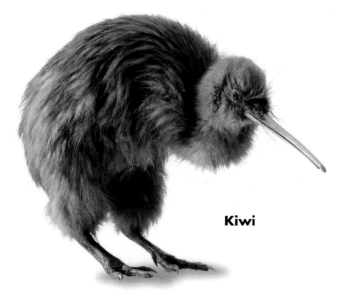

Kiwi

Can any birds swim?

Most birds can't swim.

Geese, swans, and ducks

are some birds that can.

Birds that swim usually

have webbed feet

that work like paddles.

A penguin swims and dives

with wings shaped like flippers.

Why do birds have beaks?

A bird uses its beak to get food,

carry things, and protect itself.

The shape of a bird's beak

shows us what kind of food it eats.

A hummingbird uses its long beak

like a straw to drink nectar from a flower.

Parrots have hook-shaped beaks
strong enough to crack
hard nuts and seeds.

A pelican's beak scoops fish
out of the water and holds them
in a special pouch.

Parrot

Bird beaks never stop growing.
A bird chews on hard objects,
which wears its beak down and
keeps the beak from getting too long.

Pelican

17

What do birds eat?

Birds may eat seeds, fruit, nuts,
insects, fish, or small animals.
Woodpeckers drill holes into trees
with their beaks and pull insects out
with their long, sticky tongues.
Toucans use their beaks
to pluck fruit from plants.
Owls eat small animals whole.
Then they spit up a lump
containing the animals' bones and fur.

Ivory-Billed
Woodpecker

How well do birds see?

Sight is a bird's most important sense.

A peregrine falcon can spot a mouse

one mile away while flying very fast.

Penguins see very well in water,

but not as well on land.

A bird's eyes are usually

on the sides of its head.

Each eye sees something different.

This helps birds find food

and avoid predators at the same time.

20

An owl's eyes face forward and
are on the front of its head.
Owls have to turn their heads around
to look in other directions.
Their large eyes let in lots of light,
so they can see well at night.

Why do birds build nests?

Birds build nests to lay their eggs in
and to protect their young.
A female bird usually builds the nest
with twigs, sticks, moss, grass,
or whatever she can find.
Some birds weave the pieces together.
Others stick them together with mud.
Nests are built in trees, barns,
ponds, and in many other places.

One of the biggest nests

was built by bald eagles in Florida.

It was nine feet wide!

Not all birds make nests.

Wild parrots lay eggs in holes

they find in trees or in the ground.

Birds use their nests until their

young can care for themselves.

How are baby birds born?

All birds hatch from eggs

laid by a mother bird.

One or both of the parents sits on the eggs

to keep them warm

until they are ready to hatch.

This warming time is called

incubation (enk-yu-BAY-shun).

The bigger a bird's egg is,

the longer it usually incubates.

An egg may incubate for as little

as ten days or as long as eighty days.

A male emperor penguin

carries an egg on its feet

for sixty-five days while it incubates.

Emperor Penguin

How do baby birds grow?

A newborn bird is called a chick.

When they are born, most chicks

don't have feathers and can't see.

Their parents must bring them food

and keep them warm.

Some parents swallow food,

then bring it back to the nest

and spit it up for their chicks to eat.

Most birds become fledglings (FLEJ-lings)

when they are between

two and ten weeks old.

This means they grow strong feathers
and are ready to learn to fly.
Not all birds need help
from their parents.
The chicks born to chickens
and some other birds can run around
within a few hours of hatching!
Birds grow to full size within a year.

Bluejays

Rainbow Lorikeets

How do birds take baths?

Many birds splash

in shallow water to bathe.

Some birds bathe in dust!

This helps remove bugs

from their feathers.

A bird also runs its beak
through its feathers
to comb, clean, and oil them.
This is called preening.
Pet birds often try to preen
their human owners' hair.

When do birds sleep?

Most birds sleep at night

and take short naps during the day.

They may sleep standing up

on one or both legs.

When a bird bends its knees,

its toes lock tightly

around a branch or perch

so it won't fall off while it sleeps.

Wild birds sometimes sleep

with one eye open

to watch for danger.

Swifts can sleep while flying!

Owls and other nocturnal birds sleep

during the day.

Flamingos

Why do birds sing?

Many birds sing to attract mates,
tell other birds who they are,
or warn enemies away.
Male birds sing much more often
than females do.
Most singing birds can't sing well
unless other birds teach them
when they are young.

Chicks listen to their parents sing
before trying it themselves.
Each type of bird sings a different song.
Some types of birds can learn
only one song.
Canaries keep adding new notes
to their songs all their lives.
Mockingbirds can copy the songs
of other birds.

Canary

Parakeets

Can birds really talk?

Many parrots and parakeets can
repeat words or sounds they hear.
They can't make up words,
and must hear the same
sound or word often
before they learn to say it.
Some birds can copy the
sound of a whistle, siren,
or ringing phone.

To train a pet bird to talk,

begin by repeating a single word

several times a day.

Practice when it's quiet and

you are alone with your bird.

You might start by teaching

your bird to say its name.

After it learns that, you can

slowly add more words.

Once a bird is able to speak

its first word clearly,

it will learn new words more easily.

Parrot

Are birds smart?

Most birds are smart.

A pet bird may figure out how
to unlatch its cage.

It might learn to hop up
a bird ladder or ring a bell.

People have taught their birds
to play a simple game of tag.

Some parrots have been trained
to play a short song on a piano
or to ride a bird-sized bike.

What jobs can birds do?

Homing pigeons can travel
quickly over long distances
and then return home again.
Ancient Greeks used pigeon messengers
to send news about the Olympic Games.

A pigeon named Dear Friend
received a medal for delivering
important messages to an army
in World War I.
A written message was rolled up
inside a tiny tube tied to
the bird's leg with string.

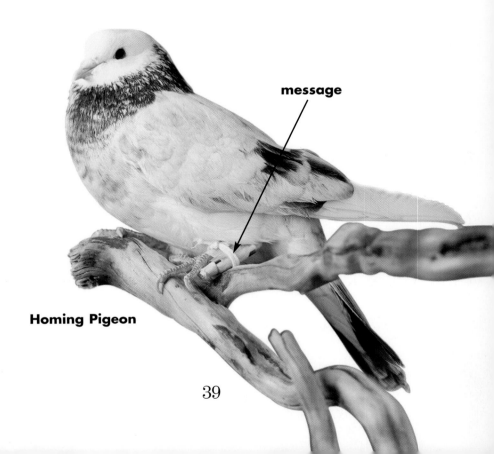

message

Homing Pigeon

Horned Puffins

Zebra Finches

Do birds like to be with other birds?

Birds can get lonely without
other birds or people around.
Parakeets, finches, and other birds
may like to live in pairs or groups.
Some birds want to be
in a cage alone.
Many wild birds live together
in groups called flocks.
Pet birds sometimes think their owners
are part of their flock.

Are pet birds easy to take care of?

Birds need food, water, shelter, friendship, and veterinary care. Pet birds can be messy. They drop feathers, dust, and poop. Their cages must be cleaned often.

Birds need a cage with enough space
to exercise their wings.
Some pet birds like to be let out
of their cages to fly in a large, safe area.
You should never leave a pet bird alone
when it is out of its cage
or let it fly freely outdoors.
Get an adult's permission
before releasing your bird.

Do birds like toys?

Pet birds need safe toys
for fun and exercise.
Most birds like toys
they can hold and
toys that dangle or twirl.
They also may like shiny,
colorful, or noisy toys.

Many birds will play

on a swing or ladder.

Parakeets like to look

at themselves in a mirror.

They think they are seeing another bird.

Birds get bored with old toys

and need a new toy now and then.

How can I make a bird feeder?

You can turn a pinecone

into a bird feeder.

First, tie a string to the top

of a large pinecone.

Spread peanut butter

all over the pinecone, then roll it

in birdseed until the peanut butter

is covered with seeds.

Hang your bird feeder

on a tree branch outdoors.

Watch from an inside window

to see if birds visit your feeder!

Pet birds can be

loving and playful.

Each bird is a little different.

Find out what your bird

likes and needs.

Be a good friend to your bird

and it will be a good friend to you.